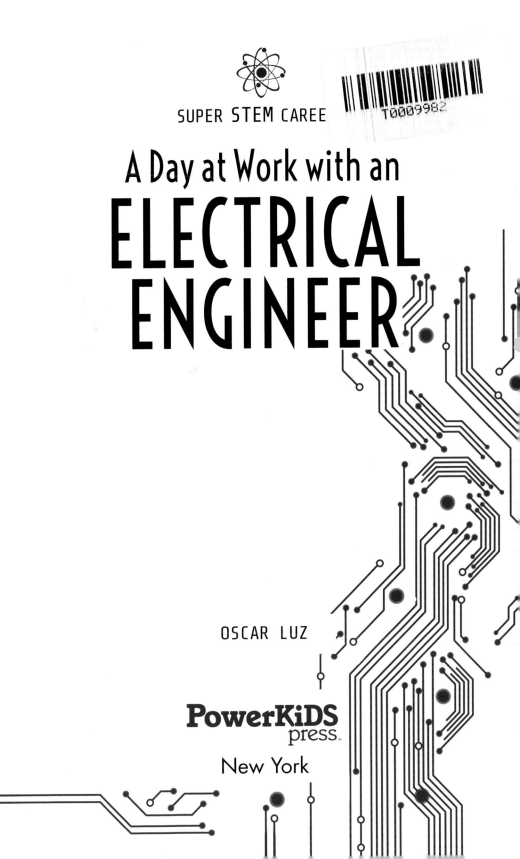

SUPER STEM CAREE

A Day at Work with an
ELECTRICAL
ENGINEER

OSCAR LUZ

PowerKiDS press.

New York

Published in 2016 by The Rosen Publishing Group, Inc.
29 East 21st Street, New York, NY 10010

First Edition

Editor: Caitie McAneney
Book Design: Katelyn Heinle/Reann Nye

Photo Credits: Cover Bulent Esdogan/thinkstockphotos.com; cover, pp. 1, 3, 4, 6, 8–10, 12–16, 18–24 (circuit vector design) VLADGRIN/Shutterstock.com; p. 5 (top) ronstik/Shutterstock.com; p. 5 (bottom) Hulton Archive/Getty Images; p. 7 (top) Settaphan Rummanee/Shutterstock.com; p. 7 (bottom) Lefteris Papaulakis/Shutterstock.com; p. 8 MilanB/Shutterstock.com; p. 9 hramovnick/Shutterstock.com; p. 11 (top) Hugo Felix/Shutterstock.com; p. 11 (bottom) Teodora D/Shutterstock.com; p. 12 leo_photo/Shutterstock.com; p. 13 MilanMarkovic78/Shutterstock.com; p. 15 Goodluz/Shutterstock.com; p. 17 (top) Marcin Krzyzak/Shutterstock.com; p. 17 (bottom) joingate/Shutterstock.com; p. 19 ratmaner/Shutterstock.com; p. 20 michaeljung/Shutterstock.com; p. 22 Echo/Cultura/Getty Images.

Library of Congress Cataloging-in-Publication Data

Luz, Oscar, author.
 A day at work with an electrical engineer / Oscar Luz.
     pages cm. — (Super STEM careers)
 Includes index.
ISBN 978-1-5081-4422-9 (pbk.)
ISBN 978-1-5081-4423-6 (6 pack)
ISBN 978-1-5081-4424-3 (library binding)
1. Electrical engineering—Vocational guidance—Juvenile literature. 2. Electrical engineers—Juvenile literature. I. Title.
TK159.L89 2016
621.3—dc23
                                2015034693

Manufactured in the United States of America

CPSIA Compliance Information: Batch #BW16PK: For Further Information contact Rosen Publishing, New York, New York at 1-800-237-9932

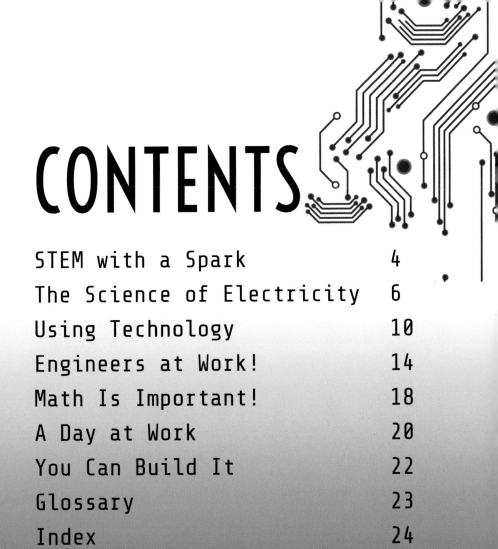

CONTENTS

STEM WITH A SPARK

Do you like to take electronics apart and see how they work? Do you have a great idea for a new electrical device, such as a phone or TV? If so, you might be interested in a career in electrical engineering.

Electrical engineers **design** and build all kinds of electrical devices, from lighting systems to smartphones. They use electricity to create inventions that make our lives easier and more fun. Today, electrical engineers are focused on finding and using clean sources of electricity. They're also masters of STEM, which stands for "science, **technology**, **engineering**, and math."

SUPER STEM SMARTS

One of the first electrical engineers was Benjamin Franklin. In 1752, he experimented with electricity by tying a key to a kite in a lightning storm. The lightning electrified the key, proving there was electricity present.

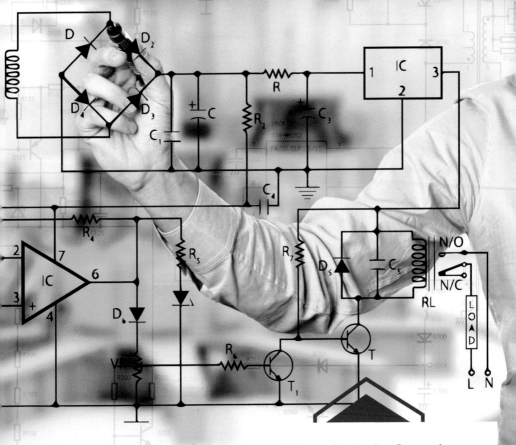

This electrical engineer is drawing a diagram of an electrical circuit.

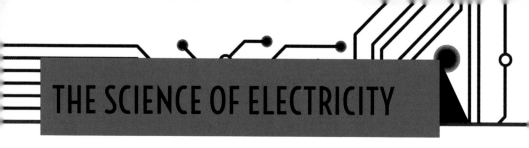

THE SCIENCE OF ELECTRICITY

Electrical engineers are masters of using electricity to make something new. It's important that they understand how electricity works.

Electricity is a kind of energy. When electricity builds up in one space, it's called static electricity. When it moves through something, it's called current electricity. Current electricity is used to power electrical devices, such as lamps and computers.

Electricity can be used to create motion. You can see this in action if you look at a fan. Motion can also turn into electricity if you have a **generator**.

SUPER STEM SMARTS

Electricity flows well through certain **materials**. Electrical engineers often use copper wire to **conduct** electricity.

circuit board

A circuit is a closed path an electric current can flow through. A circuit board is a thin board that holds an electric circuit.

circuit diagram

What do magnets and electricity have to do with each other? Each of them can create the other! If a magnetic field around a metal object—such as a copper wire—changes in strength or position, an electric current is created in the wire. However, if the magnetic field stays the same, no current is created.

An electric current in a wire also creates a magnetic field around the wire. This field can be used to push and pull magnets to create movement. This connection between a current and a magnetic field is called electromagnetism.

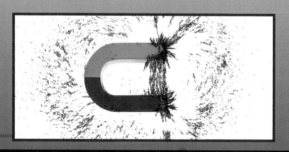

SUPER STEM SMARTS

A magnetic field is the area where a magnet has an **influence** on the metal things around it. The magnetic object can pull something to it or push it away.

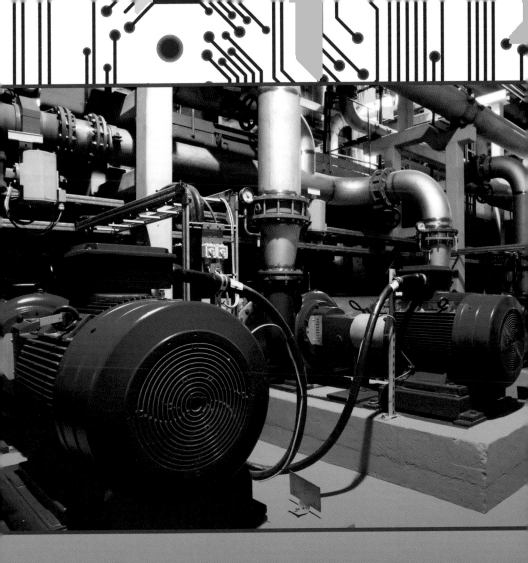

When you start a motor, electricity creates a magnetic field around wires inside the motor. This field affects nearby magnets. Together, the electricity and magnets cause parts to spin, creating movement.

USING TECHNOLOGY

Electrical engineers are the creators of the newest technology. Throughout the history of electricity, these engineers have created everything from the light bulb to the smartphone. We owe many of our everyday tools and devices to them. But what tools do electrical engineers use to do their job?

Electrical engineers use many small tools to do their job. They often work with copper wire because copper conducts electricity very well. They use needle-nose pliers to bend and shape the wire. Wire strippers are tools that help take the **insulation** off copper wire. Electrical engineers also use tweezers to grasp wire.

SUPER STEM SMARTS
Electrical engineers often use special tape that insulates wire.

The tiny tools in an electrical engineer's toolbox can help them make repairs and rewire an electrical system.

needle-nose pliers

Electrical engineers also use devices that are larger and more advanced. They often need to take measurements of electricity. For this, they may use an oscilloscope. This device measures the **frequency** of an electrical signal over time. The device produces an image of the signal in a wave graph.

Sometimes electrical engineers have to join two parts together. If the parts are metal, they use a soldering iron. Soldering irons use electricity to create heat, which helps engineers apply a special paste to the object they're working on.

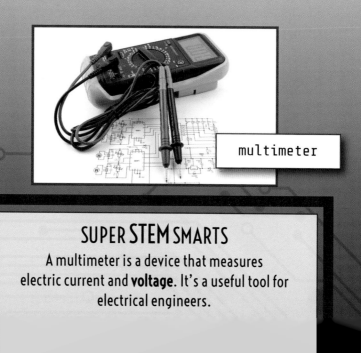

multimeter

SUPER STEM SMARTS
A multimeter is a device that measures electric current and **voltage**. It's a useful tool for electrical engineers.

This electrical engineer is using a voltmeter to measure the voltage of a device.

ENGINEERS AT WORK!

Electrical engineers may spend their workday repairing and **troubleshooting** electrical devices and systems. However, many also design new devices or improve old ones. After all, engineers are people who create new technology!

Electrical engineers usually focus on one kind of device. Some design electrical systems that power buildings, houses, and even entire factories. Some design devices that help people communicate and stay informed, such as cell phones and radio systems. Others may get an idea for a household device that will make life easier for people. They may design a new kind of blender, alarm system, or vacuum cleaner.

SUPER STEM SMARTS

Electrical engineers try to use the best materials in their designs to make their products good quality, yet inexpensive. They also look for ways to use less energy to power a device.

Today, electrical engineers are looking for ways to power devices using clean energy, such as solar, or sun, power. Some engineers even design the solar panels that generate electricity.

Some electrical engineers work on devices so small they're called microelectronics. These engineers design and build tiny parts for electronic circuits. Even though the parts are tiny, they're an important part of any electronic device, from tablets to huge factory machines.

Electrical engineers who design and create new computer technology are called computer engineers. They come up with new ways for computers to be more user-friendly. They create the hardware, or the actual computer. Some design huge supercomputers that help scientists do experiments and keep large amounts of information. Others create small tablets you can keep in your book bag.

SUPER STEM SMARTS

In the future, electronic engineers may work on creating devices that communicate with each other. For example, a "smart road" would send a message to your "smart car" telling it to slow down.

Look around your house. Think of all the things electrical engineers have designed and created to make your life easier!

MATH IS IMPORTANT!

Electrical engineers have to be very precise, or exact, in their work, so it's important that they take perfect measurements. This is especially important when the engineer is making their designs. Each measurement on their design must be clear and precise so other workers called technicians can assemble the device correctly.

Electrical engineers also use algebra, which involves math statements that describe relationships between **variables**. Variables electrical engineers may work with are voltage and current. The statements, called equations, can help electrical engineers calculate the voltage and current needed to power an electrical device.

Engineers often study geometry, or the math of shapes. This helps them make the drawing for a new device.

A DAY AT WORK

Every **industry** needs electrical engineers to design and develop new tools, machines, and products. Some electrical engineers work for big electronics companies to make new devices, such as televisions and gaming systems. They may give support for customers who use the product or even repair the product.

Electrical engineers may spend a lot of time in their office designing parts and devices and **simulating** their use on computers. They also test the materials and devices in a lab. Many labs have rooms or tools that reach very low or very high temperatures to test their products.

Electrical engineers sometimes work on a project with a team of engineers. They have to be good at communicating with team members.

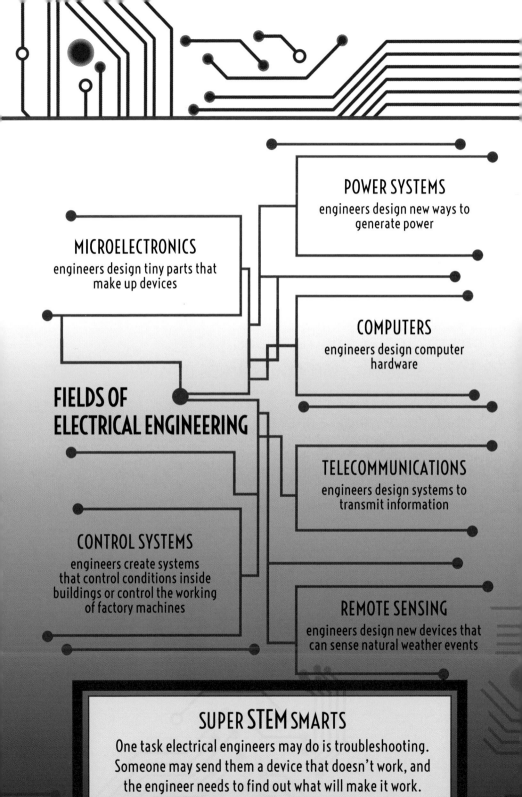

POWER SYSTEMS
engineers design new ways to generate power

MICROELECTRONICS
engineers design tiny parts that make up devices

COMPUTERS
engineers design computer hardware

FIELDS OF ELECTRICAL ENGINEERING

TELECOMMUNICATIONS
engineers design systems to transmit information

CONTROL SYSTEMS
engineers create systems that control conditions inside buildings or control the working of factory machines

REMOTE SENSING
engineers design new devices that can sense natural weather events

SUPER STEM SMARTS
One task electrical engineers may do is troubleshooting. Someone may send them a device that doesn't work, and the engineer needs to find out what will make it work.

YOU CAN BUILD IT

To become an electrical engineer, you need at least a bachelor's degree, which takes about four years to earn. You should study electrical engineering, computer engineering, physics, or mechanical engineering. Many electrical engineers gain advanced degrees in one area of study, such as microelectronics or computers.

You can start your career now by paying attention in your science and math classes. In high school, take as many STEM classes as you can. You can even safely study your electronics at home. As an electrical engineer, if you have an idea, you can build it!

GLOSSARY

conduct: To allow heat or electricity to travel along or through.

design: To create the plan for something. Also, the plan for something.

engineering: The use of science and math to build better objects.

frequency: The number of times that something (such as a wave) is repeated in a period of time.

generator: A machine that uses moving parts to produce electrical energy.

industry: A group of businesses that provide a certain product or service.

influence: An effect one thing has on another.

insulation: Something that stops heat, electricity, or sound from going into or out of a material.

material: Something used to make something else.

simulate: To represent the operation of a process by means of another system, such as a computer.

technology: The way people do something using tools and the tools that they use.

troubleshoot: To work to locate the cause of problems and make needed repairs.

variable: A quantity that may change when other conditions change.

voltage: The force of an electrical current.

INDEX

WEBSITES

Due to the changing nature of Internet links, PowerKids Press has developed an online list of websites related to the subject of this book. This site is updated regularly. Please use this link to access the list: www.powerkidslinks.com/ssc/elec